THE BLONDE AND OTHER SLIGHT DISTRACTIONS

A collection of one-acts

By

David L. Paterson

SAMUEL FRENCH, INC.

45 West 25th Street
NEW YORK 10010
LONDON

7623 Sunset Boulevard
HOLLYWOOD 90046
TORONTO

Copyright © 2005 by David L. Paterson

IMPORTANT BILLING AND CREDIT
REQUIREMENTS

All producers of **THE BLONDE AND OTHER DISTRACTIONS** must give credit to the Author of the Play in all programs distributed in connection with performances of the Play, and in all instances in which the title of the Play appears for the purposes of advertising, publicizing or otherwise exploiting the Play and /or a production. The name of the Author must appear on a separate line on which no other name appears, immediately following the title and must appear in size of type not less than fifty percent of the size of the title type.

CONTENTS

THE BLONDE 7

THANKSGETTING 21

FINAL APPROACH 29

CLOSURE 37

ONE LAST TIME 43

THE GATE 49

THE BLONDE

THE BLONDE

The Blonde was first produced as a staged reading by Food For
Thought Productions
starring
Austin Pendelton and Laila Robins

The Blonde premiered February 7th, 2004
at
The Blue Heron Theatre,
123 East 24th Street, NYC
Produced by Third Avenue Productions
Directed by Jeffrey David Stocker
Starring Kevin T. Collins and Kristen Moser

The action takes place in a dusty, windowless
concrete room.

Characters:
Eddie
Gloria

(Lights up on a stark, cement-block bunker. A heavy door swings open as EDDIE, a stocky, clumsy looking man enters with a loaded handcart. Standing on the cart, covered in a blanket, is a body. Eddie wheels the cart over to a single chair in the room and stops. He helps the wrapped figure sit down in the chair and he puts the handcart in the corner, He flips on an overlight bulb and removes the blanket, revealing GLORIA, a pleasant looking woman in her thirties. She is bound and gagged.)

EDDIE. I figure we should get some things straight. Now — this room is solid concrete. The ceilings — reinforced and soundproofed. If you scream, you'll just be hurting your voice. No one will hear you. Above ground, there are no houses, nothing. Do you understand?

(GLORIA nods.)

EDDIE. So, I'm going to take off the handkerchief. Okay?

(EDDIE cautiously takes off the bandanna and jumps back, covering his ears. GLORIA looks at him blankly.)

GLORIA. What are you doing?
EDDIE. I thought you were going to scream.
GLORIA. You said it was pointless.
EDDIE. Yeah. I know, but I thought you might try.
GLORIA. Why?
EDDIE. I don't know — I just thought —
GLORIA. You thought? Don't hurt yourself.
EDDIE. What?
GLORIA. So what's on the menu for today? Is it me? Then let's get it over with.
EDDIE. Huh?
GLORIA. If you'd loosen the ropes around my ankles, I'll spread my legs as far as possible, but please don't tear the panties — they're brand new and I'm kind of partial to them.
EDDIE. What?
GLORIA.The panties — Liz Clairborne. I like them a lot. So let's go big boy.
EDDIE. I...
GLORIA. Or are you a small boy? We can do it twice if that will make you feel better.

EDDIE. No...
GLORIA. Good, once is fine for me.

(EDDIE looks around the room, confused.)

GLORIA. No condoms? I have a couple in my purse. Make a choice but I prefer the double-ribbed fiberflex.
EDDIE. No —
GLORIA. No condom? Sure if you want to take the risk — I might just have a big hairy disease that'll snap your pecker off —
EDDIE. I —
GLORIA. Don't have all day? Neither do I, so let's go...COME ON!
EDDIE. Why are you being so mean to me?
GLORIA. How's that?
EDDIE. I just want to talk.
GLORIA. It's funny you should mention that because this is how I attend all my cocktail parties. Kidnapped from a shopping mall parking lot and spend the evening tied up with gaffers tape discussing the ozone and global trouble spots. Do I look like I was brought in with today's paper? Wise up Franklin.
EDDIE. My name's Eddie.
GLORIA. Okay Munster — Just do me and lets get this over with.
EDDIE. I don't want to "do" you.
GLORIA. Oh that's right — you're the talker. What? The plumbing don't work?
EDDIE. What?
GLORIA. Leaky balloon?
EDDIE. What?
GLORIA. Habla ingles?
EDDIE. Yes.
GLORIA. So you're not stupid!
EDDIE. No, I'm not stupid... when I was born I was a bit slow. The doctors diagnosed me as an "idiot savant." But when I was five I got upgraded to idiot. Actually, I just didn't have much to say.
GLORIA. You're tearin' my heart out, chico.
EDDIE. It's Eddie.
GLORIA. Munster.
EDDIE. Cheese...
GLORIA.Whiz...
EDDIE. What?

GLORIA. Look, Mr. Esposito, I'm almost as calm as I will be, so — see me as I am — use me as you will.

(She leans her head back and slips out of her shoes.)

EDDIE. What's your favorite color?

GLORIA. Blue, Okay?!! Do me!

EDDIE. Do what?

GLORIA. Jeez — do I have to paint a picture?

EDDIE. Would you like to? I can get some stuff.

GLORIA. God, I'm trapped in a bunker with Rainman.

EDDIE. It's Eddie...Why are you so angry?

GLORIA. When you wake up in the morning — do you have to turn on a switch up there?

EDDIE. Up where?

GLORIA. Why are you doing this to me?

EDDIE. I thought we could talk.

GLORIA. Is this how you usually date?

EDDIE. No.

GLORIA. Cause I think it's illegal.

EDDIE. I think so, yes.

GLORIA. So, why'd you take me?

EDDIE. I don't know... I saw you come out of that Walmart...the sun caught your hair... you seemed so confident.

GLORIA. I was buying tampons.

EDDIE. I just wanted to meet you... I didn't think you'd —

GLORIA. Volunteer to be jumped from behind, stuffed in a sleeping bag, hog tied and tossed in a car and dragged kicking and screaming to Jeffrey Dahmer's basement?

EDDIE. I'm not going to eat you.

GLORIA. Well now, I can relax.

EDDIE. Please do...

GLORIA. I'm relaxed. Can I go now?

EDDIE. Well...

GLORIA. You're really putting a cramp in my day, here.

EDDIE. Sorry...

GLORIA. So why me? You had a whole shopping mall to choose from... look at me. I'm not even blonde.

EDDIE. It was the moment, I just... didn't want you to get away... before we get a chance to talk... It's not my fault... you made me love you.

GLORIA. Oh, I know that one *(Singing.)* "You made me love you, I didn't want to do it, I didn't want to do it. You made me kill your dog — and all the time you knew it — cut out his brain and chewed it." C'mon that's the top stalker song of all time.

EDDIE. I never heard of it.

GLORIA. How about deodorant? Ever heard of that?

EDDIE. You're mean.

GLORIA. Well, I've had a bad day.

EDDIE. What do you do?

GLORIA. When I'm not tied up?

EDDIE. Do you have a job?

GLORIA. I'm a mammalian lifeguard.

EDDIE. A what?

GLORIA. I teach lemmings how to swim.

EDDIE. ...No you don't.

GLORIA. Ah, you can see right through me — all three-hundred and seventy-six pounds.

EDDIE. You're not fat. You're perfect.

GLORIA. That means a lot — coming from you. What are you, a Postal Worker?

EDDIE. No... a handy man.

GLORIA. I'll bet.

EDDIE. What do you do... really?

GLORIA. I'm a statistician.

EDDIE. ...You're a baby doctor?

GLORIA. That's an obstetrician, I'm a statistician.

EDDIE. ...You check babies for static?

GLORIA. I compile, analyze and organize various bits of worthless and semi-worthless trivial data for specific organizations and companies throughout this great land of ours.

EDDIE. You work for Jeopardy?

GLORIA. Yeah — I nailed Alex Trebec just last month.

EDDIE. Nailed?

GLORIA. Did you eat concrete as a child?

EDDIE. No.

GLORIA. What are we doing here, Eddie?

EDDIE. Talking.

GLORIA. For the purpose of?

EDDIE. Getting to know each other.

GLORIA. And then?

EDDIE. And then... what?

GLORIA. You tell me — I'm a little in the dark here.

EDDIE. I could get a brighter bulb.

GLORIA. ... When the ship left for planet retard, did they just forget to pick you up?

EDDIE. *(Quietly.)* I'm not retarded.

GLORIA. Did I say you were?

EDDIE. You said the people from planet retard forgot to take me back.

GLORIA. I didn't say back — you could just be visiting.

EDDIE. I got the point.

GLORIA. You gonna kill me or what?

EDDIE. Or what.

GLORIA. What?

EDDIE. I'm not going to kill you... so I guess it's "or what."

GLORIA. So you are going to let me go.

EDDIE. If I have to.

GLORIA. Have to - what do you mean have to? Like if the cops find me, or what?

EDDIE. Or what.

GLORIA. Oh boy.

EDDIE. I'll let you go if this doesn't work out.

GLORIA. What doesn't work out?

EDDIE. Our relationship.

GLORIA. Our relationship?

EDDIE. Yes.

GLORIA. Well, let me save you a bit of frustration. There is no way on God's green earth or this dump basement that we are going to establish any kind of relationship, so why don't you let me go?

EDDIE. Okay... All you have to do -

GLORIA. Ah — here we go — what is it? The banana down the throat trick?

EDDIE. No..

GLORIA. Spit it out Eddie.

EDDIE. All you have to do is say Peggy Babcock, five times really fast.

GLORIA. You gotta be kidding.

EDDIE. No.

GLORIA. Peggy Babcock?

EDDIE. Five times.

GLORIA. Fast.

EDDIE. Real fast.

GLORIA. Right... and then I can go.
EDDIE. Yes.
GLORIA. Okay, here it goes... Peggy Babcock — Peggy Babcock — Peggy Babcock — Peggy Babcock — Hagey Babecock
EDDIE. Hagey Babecock?
GLORIA. I didn't say that, I said Peggy Babcock... Can I try it again?
EDDIE. No.
GLORIA. Well that wasn't fair! You made it sound simple!
EDDIE. I am simple.
GLORIA. I'm going to leave that one alone. Please Eddie, give me another chance. Look, if you're thinking about the relationship thing, I gotta tell you — I am awful. Awful. I haven't been in a relationship since my therapist and that was years ago.
EDDIE. We can take our time.
GLORIA. Eddie, I don't think my circulation will last that long.
EDDIE. Oh.

(EDDIE removes the gaffer tape from her legs. He produces a pair of handcuffs and cuffs her leg to the chair.)

GLORIA. God, you're romantic.
EDDIE. You think?
GLORIA. No.

(EDDIE removes the tape from her wrists and steps back.)

EDDIE. How's that?
GLORIA. It's better.
EDDIE. Are you hungry?
GLORIA. No.
EDDIE. Thirsty?
GLORIA. No. Tired? No. Horny? No. Angry? Getting there.
EDDIE. I wrote a poem.
GLORIA. You want me to check out your longfellow?
EDDIE. You want to hear it?
GLORIA. If it ends with me walkin out that door, than yes.
EDDIE. Oh... it doesn't.
GLORIA. You know, you seem so gentle...so kind. How could the man that writes poetry be as cruel as this?
EDDIE. I don't mean to be cruel.

GLORIA. But that's what you are — what you are doing to me.

EDDIE. No -

GLORIA. What's the matter — cat got your mother?

EDDIE. Leave my mother out of this.

GLORIA. Gladly — why don't you leave me out of this, while you're at it?

EDDIE. I -

GLORIA. What? What? C'mon, spit it out. I-know it ain't a relationship you're aiming for, so what is it? What do you want?

EDDIE. A baby.

GLORIA. What?

EDDIE. I want a baby.

GLORIA . Whoa! Hang on here, Franklin. Do I look like a babe-o-matic? Pop the quarter in and - FLANK! Out pops a newborn?! You're barkin' up the wrong bush, cowboy. I am nobody's incubator — so just go ahead and snap my neck.

EDDIE. You don't like babies?

GLORIA. From a distance, in the dark, out of earshot, I think they're the bees-freakin'-knees - but I have no desire for an eighteen year millstone around my neck. I'd rather eat glass.

EDDIE. I'd take care of it.

GLORIA. In between the ball scratching — beer drinking — half-time breaks, maybe. Do you even have a job?

EDDIE. I'd take care of it completely.

GLORIA. Buddy — you can't — it's as simple as that. You think you can raise a child in this world. The chances and odds are completely against it. First of all — you got to get the gremlin out of the oven in one piece. Now I'm in my thirties, so I'd have to get an amnio, now there's a one in seven hundred chance it'll be born with eight foreheads because of that. Besides my eggs are a bit on the well-done side anyway. So for all we know we'd have a baby with a beard. If it gets your brain then he'll get the shit kicked out of him on the playground every damn day. Now fifty to seventy-five percent of all new mothers experience varying degrees of postpartum depression. Some mothers experience psychosis, that's one in one thousand, in the first two weeks after the birth. So you could be out of the room for just a flash — next thing you know, I'm trying to stuff the gremlin in my mouth like some over-worked hamster.

 EDDIE. They do that?

GLORIA. You bet your ass — toots.

EDDIE. So, I'll be extra careful.

GLORIA. God, you're clueless. If you let him outside the house, I give him a week before he's dead.

EDDIE. He?

GLORIA. He, she, it. Doesn't matter. If it survives infancy it'll be taken out in school, Almost three million crimes occur on or near school property every year. That's sixteen thousand a day - one every six seconds. One in five students carry some form of weapon and one in twenty carries a gun. One fourth of major urban school districts use metal detectors for weapon searches. And the number of young Americans killed by firearms each year has doubled in the last twenty years.

EDDIE. Maybe we should consider private school.

GLORIA. Catholic?

EDDIE. Okay.

GLORIA. Next thing you know our kid's getting a tonsillectomy from the head priest. Look ma - no hands!

EDDIE. We could teach at home. I'd like that. Then we could play - watch T.V., learn to ride a bike -

GLORIA. Hold on Jose! Do you know how many injuries take place around the home?

EDDIE. No.

GLORIA.Well, me neither, but it's a buttload. And how about kiddie T.V., huh? Thirty-two violent acts per hour, fifty-six percent of the characters are violent. Seventy-four percent are characters who are victims of violence, and seventy-nine percent are characters involved in violence either as perpetrators or victims!

EDDIE. Wow.

GLORIA. I'm just getting warm here, spanky. Let's move on to that bike bit. Every year, fifty thousand kids under the age of fifteen suffer head injuries, one thousand seriously every day.

EDDIE. Wow.

GLORIA. Four hundred a year bite it. And that's just from the bikes. Before nightfall, forty thousand kids will die from whatever. Fifty-five in the next thirty seconds.

EDDIE. From what?

GLORIA. Mostly malnutrition and disease.

EDDIE. Okay, no T.V., must wear a helmet, three meals a day and all vaccines taken care of early on.

GLORIA. Oh Eddie, Eddie, Eddie. If we get him through puberty, he's definitely going out then. If it's a boy — he'll knock somebody up — a girl — pregoville. Fifty-four percent of freshmen in high school do it and seventy-two percent of seniors on a semi-regular basis.

EDDIE. We could teach our child responsibility.

GLORIA. You're referring, of course, to the over one-hundred-million acts of sexual intercourse taking place daily resulting in about nine hundred ten thousand conceptions and three-hundred-fifty thousand cases of sexually transmitted diseases.

EDDIE. Eew.

GLORIA. Eew is right, poppa-daddy. And let's say he makes it to college — you want the drop-out rate or the no-shows?

EDDIE. Neither.

GLORIA. Fine - let's say he makes it to the real world. We're talking about a country where eighty percent of the population live on two percent of the land. If you walk on the street or go to the post office you'll get your head blown off. By the way — twenty five thousand people were murdered last year. Every twenty-two seconds somebody is shot, strangled or stabbed to death. That probably has something to do with the large number of available handguns.

(Eddie removes Gloria's handcuffs. She stands, but continues to lecture, ignoring her freedom.)

GLORIA. And what kind of country would the kid live in? During the eighties, sixty percent of Americans thought they would be better off than their parents. Today, it's twenty-five percent. Americans improperly dispose more than four hundred million gallons of oil a year -about thirty-five times more than the Exxon Valdez!

(Eddie opens the door and stands by it, dejectedly.)

GLORIA. Of course, he'd probably die of lack of oxygen from the deforestaion of the Planet. You know there's only about five percent of virgin forest left here untouched in the U.S.?

EDDIE. I did not know that.

GLORIA. Did I mention we're losing an acre a minute of the Amazon Rain Forest?

EDDIE. You did now.

GLORIA. Then again, all of this worrying is for nothing anyway.

EDDIE. It is?

GLORIA. Yeah...Because we're all going to be taken out any day anyway. You see, on March 23, 1989, an asteroid, half a mile wide just missed the earth by seven hundred thousand miles. Now, by astronomical calculations, we were damn lucky. If it had arrived on its trajectory six hours later, it could have wiped out the whole planet.

(EDDIE sits down next to the door.)

GLORIA. What's the matter?
EDDIE. You can go... I'm sorry I took you.
GLORIA. You're letting me go?
EDDIE. Yes.
GLORIA. You want me to try to say Peggy Babcock again?
EDDIE. No.
GLORIA. So, I'm not good enough for you?
EDDIE. It's not that.
GLORIA. Is it my thighs? I've been working on them.
EDDIE You're right... no reason to bring a child into the world.
GLORIA. So it's not me?
EDDIE. It's the planet.
GLORIA. I'm glad you see my point... I just wanted you to know what you're up against.
EDDIE. Yeah...
GLORIA. I guess I can be a downer. I can get a little maniacle.
EDDIE. No, I took those off.
GLORIA. No — I meant, crazy.
EDDIE. Sorry about taking you.
GLORIA. Oh — that's okay...it's just — maybe you should have asked.
EDDIE. Definitely.
GLORIA. Look... I got to get back to work... but...

(She picks up her purse and opens it, producing a card.)

GLORIA. Why don't you give me a call.
EDDIE. What for?
GLORIA. For dinner.
EDDIE. What's the point?
GLORIA. Well, there's always a point for dinner. It's to suppress hunger and replace nutrients... Well, think about it.
EDDIE. Okay.

(Gloria walks to the door and pauses.)

GLORIA. I had a great time.
EDDIE. Hm.
GLORIA. I'll see you later. Maybe?

(Eddie dejectedly nods as Gloria starts to exit.)

GLORIA. You know it's nice to meet a man who really can listen...there's something very special about that... course by the age of seventy five you'll probably suffer from up to thirty percent hearing loss due to octical neuron degeneration of the inner ear, but, uh, that's not for awhile... anyway.. .I can stay if —

*(Eddie closes the door in her face and picks up some rope, making a noose
and prepares to throw the rope over something on the ceiling as the lights
fade to black.)*

(BLACKOUT)

THE END

THE BLONDE AND OTHER
SLIGHT DISTRACTIONS

THANKSGETTING

THANKSGETTING

Thanksgetting was a winner of
The Lebanon Theater 2002 Playwriting Contest

Thanksgetting premiered
at
The Lebanon Theater
August 16th, 2002
Directed by Chet Rittle
Featuring John Kelsey and Ken Skelly

Thanksgetting was first produced in New York City,
November 17th, 2003
at
The Players Club
16 Grammercy Park South, NYC 10003
Directed By Sarala Dee
featuring
Chris Gannon and D.L. Paterson

The author will allow the gender of the roles to change
where casting merits it.
The two characters can be two males or two females
or a combination of both.

Action takes place in an empty restaurant.

Characters:
Jim/ Jaime
Allen/ Alex

(Lights up on stage. Down center is an elegantly set table with 2 chairs. A faint knock is heard stage right. JIM enters from SL dressed in a suit and crosses off right followed by the sound of a door opening.)

JIM. *(OS.)* Hi. Come on in.

(JIM enters followed by ALLEN, a filthy street vagrant wearing several layers or heavy clothing. ALLEN looks around.)

ALLEN. Where is everybody?
JIM. I sent the staff home early, after the lunch crowd. Some had to travel I wanted to give them a head start. *(ALLEN nods slowly scanning the room.)*
ALLEN. New paint?
JIM. Well, we did it last may — but its been a year since you were here last — so , yes, it's new... please sit down.

(ALLEN sits at the table.)

JIM. *(Continued.)* You want me to take your coat?

(ALLEN stands and takes off his coat, revealing another heavy coat underneath. He hands the 1st to JIM to points at the 2nd coat.)

JIM. Do you want me to take —
ALLEN. No.

(JIM hangs the coat on the coat rack dL and x off. He returns with a plate and a bottle of wine. He places the dish in front of ALLEN who stares at it.

JIM. Veal sorrentino. Tender veal, proscuetto, eggplant, and mushrooms, in a wine sauce with freshly made mozzarella.
ALLEN. ...Well, I'll be crapping this out in about 20 minutes... could you possibly get me anything richer?... Its' fine... do you have any bread? That'll help stop me up at least.
JIM. Sure

(JIM EXITS. ALLEN takes some of the silverware and slips it into his coat pocket. He lifts the bottle and examines the label as Jim re enters with a

bowl of bread.)

JIM. It's a Beaujolais.
ALLEN. I can read
Jim. 74. A good year.
ALLEN. Not for Nixon.

(He pours himself a glass)

ALLEN. You want one?
JIM. Sure

(JIM sits as ALLEN pours him a glass, takes a deep swig and begins to eat.)

JIM. It was lucky I ran into you outside Grand Central last week. So we could do this tonight... I'm sorry we won't be open tomorrow but I decided this year I wanted to give the staff Thanksgiving off... I would've felt bad if you showed up tomorrow and no one was here — just some lame note taped to the door.
ALLEN. I woulda just let myself in... punched window or somethin... just kidding... what are you doing tomorrow?
JIM. Tarrytown... with Deb's folks.
ALLEN. How is Deb?
JIM. Good... she's good.
ALLEN. She's done with Chemo?
JIM. Yeah
ALLEN. And?
JIM. She seems to be doing pretty good. She's in remission.
ALLEN. ... cancer sucks...
JIM. ...yeah... it does...
ALLEN. You still live in the city?
JIM. Yep... rent control. I'm not gonna give that up... are you, uh-
ALLEN. In between residencies? Yeah. The current Administration kind of discourages us from staying in one place too long. And when your bed starts to smell more like piss than your piss, its time to move on... who made this, Carlo?
JIM. No, he uh, left. Works for Tavern on the Green now.
ALLEN. Ah, the Central Park McDonalds of the Tourist Elite.
JIM. Well, they also offer dental.
ALLEN. It's good, whoever you got now did a good job with this.

JIM. I made it.

ALLEN. ... it's a little heavy on the breading... but nothing criminal

JIM. How are you doing for money?

ALLEN. Bribing me won't change my mind of the breading... as long as the nickel deposit on cans stays firm — I got income...'course in Michigan it's ten cents for returnables... that's like a homeless person's Shangra La.

JIM. ... I put together a small bag of stuff for you — you don't have to take it, but it has some things you might want. Razors, toothpaste, couple of metrocards —

ALLEN. I don't need anything.

JIM. Okay

ALLEN. ... well, I'll take the metrocards

JIM. All right

(JIM hands ALLEN the metrocards then produces a business card)

JIM. And here's my card. The address is the same but my number changed — not that you need to call —

ALLEN. Do you got anymore of this Beaujolais?

(JIM puts the cards down on the table.)

JIM. 74? No, but I have an 86. Also a good year

ALLEN. Not for Christy McAuliff.

JIM. Christy—

ALLEN. Blew up in the Space Shuttle, in '86. School teacher.

JIM. Right

ALLEN. ... So... its been a year... How's the food biz?

JIM. It's been better... actually... we're probably gonna close down after New Years. Our lease is up and they plan to hike the rent... they'll probably be a Starbucks in here by March.

ALLEN. Great trash, Starbucks... So where you gonna relocate?

JIM. I don't see that happening, the city's changed....I can't keep up with the...

ALLEN. ...the what?

JIM. The flavor of the month, the ever changing nuance... the unpredictability of this city can be great when you're in your 20s and living large. But you get to be my age... with responsibilities,... the health department, liquor board... insurance, immigration. At some point it stops being fun... at all.

ALLEN. You were never in your 20s... you've been middle aged your whole life. You were working on your first ulcer in grade school.

JIM. How about letting my ulcers rest a bit... maybe you could come in from the cold for awhile.

ALLEN. What am I a spy?

JIM. I am serious. Its freezing out there.

ALLEN. Heat is highly over-rated.

JIM. I talked to Dad today.

ALLEN. Here we go.

JIM. He said you can come home anytime you want. You just have to take your medication —

ALLEN. Gee Beaver, that's' swell of Pop. Did you and Lumpy keep my room just the way I left it?

JIM. Allen —

ALLEN. I didn't come here for a fucking lecture. We had a deal, its just the meal, and that's it.

JIM. I am not lecturing.

ALLEN. Well, you are ruining my entree.

JIM. It just.. I'm tired... really tired-

ALLEN. Then take a nap. Take two. Sometimes I nap all day.

JIM. ... with Deb being so sick... and the restaurant going down... I need to concentrate on her and me... my future... I'm just afraid if this place goes... we-

ALLEN. We only see each other once a year anyway... It's not like if I miss this meal I'll starve to death. I eat more than once a year.

JIM. I'd like to think it was more that just the meal that made you come-

ALLEN. No...this is much more enjoyable than wading through a dumpster.

JIM. What I mean was-

ALLEN. I went to college — I understand subtext. But if you're looking for a hug Oprah... I just came here to eat... and I'm done.

(He pushes away the empty plate.)

JIM. That's it?

ALLEN. Unless you got dessert.

JIM. ... I'm all our of dessert

ALLEN. Then how about that Beaujolais?... For the road.

(JIM starts to head off Left.)

ALLEN. ... It was a good meal... a little heavy on the breading...

(JIM EXITS. ALLEN stares at the table then stands. He empties his pockets of the silverware and stuffs the bread in his pockets. He tosses a few crumpled bills on the table and crosses to grab his coast from the rack. He puts on the coat and crosses back to the table. He slips the bottle in his coat pocket and grabs JIM's card, folds it and picks some meant from between his teeth. As he starts off right he drops JIM's card to the floor and exits off right. After a beat he re-appears, pausing to look at the crumpled card on the floor. He picks it up and EXITS off right as the light fade to black.)

THE BLONDE AND OTHER
SLIGHT DISTRACTIONS

FINAL APPROACH

FINAL APPROACH

Final Approach was first produced
at
The Metropolitan Playhouse
July 28, 2003 in NYC
Directed By Adam Melnick
featuring
Julie Martin and Darcie Siciliano

The two characters' genders can change for casting purposes.

Action takes place in the front seat of a car

Characters:
Kate/Kyle
Stephanie/Steven

(Lights up on Stephanie and Katherine, sitting in the front seat of their car in Traffic. Stephanie tensely grips the wheel as Katherine stares blankly at the passing scenery.)

KATE. Motel 6.

STEPHANIE. No.

KATE. They leave the light on for you.

STEPHANIE. Well, then they're wasting electricity.

KATE. It looked pretty clean.

STEPH. Kathy-

KATE. I'm just checking...it's never too late you know...we can always pull away from th curb but once we're in that door-

STEPH. We discussed this already. It's too late.

KATE. I was joking.

STEPH. No, you weren't.

KATE. Okay, I wasn't.

STEPH. It'll be fine. We're right on time, we're not going to be late.

KATE. We're never late.

STEPH. That's because-

KATE. We don't want your father to burst into flames.

STEPH. He's just precise-

KATE. Anal comes to mind-

STEPH. Let's not go there.

KATE. I don't mind that he hates me-

STEPH. He doesn't hate you-

KATE. Then why does he always call me old girl?

STEPH. It's a term of affection.

KATE. For an old girl.

STEPH. He was being playful-

KATE. What about the crack about me and the Russian Revolution?

STEPH. It was a joke and it wasn't that funny.

KATE. You laughed.

STEPH. To be polite-that's all.

KATE. ... right...

STEPH. You're not old-he doesn't hate you-we'll be on time, so everything's okay.

KATE. ... peachy..

STEPH. We should stop off and get something.

KATE. I have the wine.

STEPH. Bringing alcohol to a Baldwin gathering is like bringing kerosene to a bonfire.

KATE. We could get a pound cake.

STEPH. When are you going to let that one go?

KATE. I worked really hard on that.

STEPH. They did not put in the freezer on purpose.

KATE. And when your uncle used it to knock the table leg back in it's socket?

STEPH. It worked, didn't it? So technically your pound cake saved the day.

KATE. I don't quite remember it that way.

STEPH. That's because you're old...I'M KIDDING! Remember that? We used to do it all the time.

KATE. I faintly remember that.

STEPH. I love you.

KATE. You better...

STEPH. ...you want to go over the list. One more time?

KATE. Stephanie-

STEPH. Please? Just one more time?

KATE. This is the last time-

STEPH. Fine-

KATE. Alright.

STEPH. Thank you.

KATE. Okay, shoot.

STEPH. ...Wendy-

KATE. Avoid discussions about the environment-that's an easy one.

STEPH. Sean-

KATE. The Middle East in general-c'mon, test me!

STEPH. Mark-

KATE. Obsessive-compulsive.

STEPH. John-

KATE. Manic-depressive-don't mention Christmas.

STEPH. Bob-

KATE. Catatonic-

STEPH. He just quiet... now...Carol?

KATE. Anorexic.

STEPH. Bolemic.

KATE. Really?

STEPH. She's moved on.

KATE. Okay, got it.

STEPH. Timmy-

KATE. Ankle biter-steer clear of the kiddie table.

STEPH. I'm sorry about this.

KATE. I can handle this. I see it as one of those Indian tests of the inner spirit.

STEPH. Oh really?

KATE. The way your folks keep the thermostat at 150 I'm sure the Indian sweat lodge motiff will be in full swing.

STEPH. You know how mom is about drafts.

KATE. Of course Custard would probably have survived the Little Big Horn if he set it on a major holiday and invited your relatives....

STEPH. ...You're wonderful.

KATE. For an old broad from the revolution, yes, I know.

STEPH. Uncle Carl-

KATE. The boozer.

STEPH. Uncle Joe-

KATE . The hugger, multiple times.

STEPH. I'll keep an eye on him.

KATE. Good luck.

STEPH. Alright, now the biggies... Dad

KATE. I have this one down cold. Father, the three f's-fascism, fashion and farm subsidies, avoid all three and watch the trick knee.

STEPH. I'm impressesd

KATE. I'm just warming up.

STEPH. Mom?

KATE. Compliment the hair, and take everything she says with a grain of salt and a shot of Tequila.

STEPH. She's not that bad.

KATE. Don't get me started.

STEPH. Kate-

KATE. And why is it that she must she call me Kath-er-rine. Like the effort will kill her. She knows to call me Kate-even Katy. But Kath-er-rine. It makes her sound asmatic.

STEPH. Hey, your mom-

KATE. Back off sweater girl. My side is not up torture today. That was last year. We should work on one disfunctional family at a time.

STEPH. Don't use that word. I hate that word. It's such a buzzword.

KATE. Buzzword?

STEPH. It's so over used. It's a, a playwrights word.

KATE. ...You're a playwright.

STEPH. And it pains me everytime I use it.

KATE. Then-

STEPH. Let's just drop it.

KATE. Fine.

STEPH. Fine... please be nice to Christopher this time.

KATE. I already apologised for that, even though I don't think I should!

STEPH. You told him Eeyore had Donkey cancer! You don't tell a six-year old that his favorite Winnie The Pooh character has inoperable rectal cancer!

KATE. It would explain why the damn donkey is always so cranky and his tail keeps falling off. Chemo. Carl thought it was funny and it's his damn kid. And I think everybody was a little relieved when the little non-stop Christopher finally shut up for awhile.

STEPH. He locked himself in a closet!

KATE. For a glorious twenty-five minutes-Okay-point is made. No donkey cancer.

STEPH. Let's just get through this without any major catastrophes, alright?

KATE. What qualifies as major? Just kidding...hey, Ho-Jo's!

STEPH. Stop it-I'm not pulling off! I've planned and prepared really hard how I'm going to suffer through this weekend and we're gonna do it!

KATE. Hey, I can handle it.

STEPH. I have no doubts.

KATE. And what about you?

STEPH. I HAVE DOUBTS!

KATE. Sweetheart, you're going to be fine. I'll be by your side the entire time-I'll even hold your hand if you want me to.

STEPH. That'll be a little difficult if your punching Uncle Carl in the forehead for his "Ooops, was that your buttocks?" routine.

KATE. I can handle it.

STEPH. As you do everything.

KATE. What does that mean?

STEPH. Look at you, steady as a rock. Look at me-

KATE. I'm looking at us, what am I looking for?

STEPH. I can't do this. I don't want to do this. I have nothing to show them or tell them or bragg about-

KATE. Is that what these get-togethers are about? Bragging?

STEPH. Obviously not, or I would'nt be invited.

KATE. Family gatherings are not fun, just required. Like renewing your drivers license.

STEPH. I'd just like to have something good to tell them...about me.

KATE. Don't do this to yourself...it's David, right?

STEPH. No-

KATE. Look, I know you two are competitive, but c'mon. You have to get over this. So he won a stupid prize-

STEPH. Uh. I don't think the Pulitzer is a little endeavor-

KATE. Look at you, you had a show produced Off Broadway-

STEPH. Off Bleeker. Off Bleeker. That's classified as off-off, way the hell, off-Broadway.

KATE. Well-

STEPH. And it was a staged reading.

KATE. Yes.

STEPH. There was three in the audience.

KATE. But-

STEPH. You, myself, and the janitor who had to lock up after us.

KATE. But he loved the Show!

STEPH. He slept through half of it!

KATE. No, that was thoughtful contemplation.

STEPH. He Snored!

KATE. ...once.

STEPH. I can't do this.

(Stephanie pulls the car over.)

KATE. ...That was an awful storm that night... nobody went out to see anything... you said it yourself, it was a dead umbrella night.

STEPH. *(Smiling.)* Yeah, I did...

KATE. It was a very funny line.

STEPH. It was the only funny line of the night... too bad it wasn't in the play...

KATE. I enjoyed the walk home, in the rain. We were laughing, remember?

STEPH. ...yes...

KATE. Stephanie, they're your family. Not an an audience.

STEPH. Please-

KATE. Not critics-

STEPH. Hah!

KATE. And not hangmen...

STEPH. ...right...

KATE. Just a bunch of people who are just as screwed up as you are, if not more. So, actually, more so.

STEPH. How so?

KATE. They don't have me.

(KATE strokes STEPHANIE's cheek. She screws up her courage and pulls the car back onto the road.)

STEPH. Hey-look, Comfort Inn!
KATE. Honey-
STEPH. I can handle this, Donkey cancer and all.

BLACKOUT

CLOSURE

CLOSURE

Closure was a finalist for
The Actor's Theatre of Louisville's
10 Minute Play Contest

The author will allow the genders of the characters
be changed for casting purposes as well as
changes of words in references to gender.

Action takes place at an outdoor café.

Characters:
Doug/ Dana
Scott/ Sara
Waiter / Waitress

(Lights up on SCOTT, sitting at a small table with another chair. DOUG ENTERS.)

DOUG. *(Happily.)* What's up?!
SCOTT. Hey...
DOUG. You didn't order yet, did you?
SCOTT. No, I just got here myself.
DOUG. Cool... so how's it going?
SCOTT. It's, um... okay, I guess.

(A WAITER approaches.)

WAITER. And how are we today?
SCOTT. We can't see each other anymore.
DOUG. What?
WAITER. I'll give you a few minutes.

(He EXITS.)

DOUG. Where is this coming from?
SCOTT. I just don't think we should see each other anymore.
DOUG. At all?
SCOTT. Right.
DOUG. Like till we're dead?
SCOTT. Yes...
DOUG. You can't be serious.
SCOTT. I am.
DOUG. Where is this coming from?
SCOTT. I've been thinking about it for quite some time.
DOUG. Dude-
SCOTT. Don't—don't call me dude—I hate when you call me dude.
DOUG. Scott—what's the problem here? I mean this—
SCOTT. You make me feel uncomfortable, sometimes.
DOUG. What do you mean?
SCOTT. Sometimes, when we're with others, you put me down.
DOUG. That's just stupid.
SCOTT. Oh, good, thanks a lot, I wanted to get into the name calling right off the bat.
DOUG. Name one incident—
SCOTT. Jim and Amy's party last week.

DOUG. What?

SCOTT. I came in late, remember? And you said—with seven or eight people around you, "Boss working you late, huh?"

DOUG. Hey-

SCOTT. They know I'm unemployed.

DOUG.Look, you're the one that embarrassed yourself.

SCOTT. No, you threw me off—I wasn't thinking—

(The waiter reenters.)

DOUG. You don't tell people you're having back hair removed!!

(The waiter exits.)

SCOTT. Why don't we tell the whole world?! My back was on fire, I couldn't come up with a creative lie on the spot—I guess I'm not as imaginative as you.

DOUG. I didn't come here to fight.

SCOTT. Neither did I, I came here for closure.

DOUG. Closure?

SCOTT. Yes. I didn't want to do this over the phone—even I have some spine.

DOUG. You can be all spine sometimes.

SCOTT. See—there you go again!

DOUG. Well, c'mon Scott-this is a very serious step. I don't think you've thought this out.

SCOTT. Well, that's me all over, never thinking things through!

(The waiter reenters.)

DOUG. YOU NEED ME!

WAITER. I'll just-why don't you, just wave or something when you're ready to order.

DOUG. That'll be fine. Thank you.

WAITER. Can I get drinks?

SCOTT. I'll have a bowl of vodka, please.

DOUG. He's joking. Two drafts, Anchor Steam.

SCOTT. I don't want a beer.

DOUG. What do you want, Scott?

WAITER. I think he—

DOUG. Excuse me. Scott?
SCOTT. I want a bowl of vodka.
WAITER. Could I put it in a mug, maybe?
DOUG. Sure.

(The waiter EXITS.)

SCOTT. I wanted a bowl—
DOUG. When he comes back, we'll get you a god-damn bowl, okay? But first, just listen to me.
SCOTT. That's what I do best. Listen to you, your lectures, your speeches—you know my therapist said—
DOUG. You're still seeing her?
SCOTT. Yes, from the change I scrape together collecting cans in public wastebaskets I've managed to continue to waste my money trying to get a grip on my very sad and stationary life.
DOUG. Scott— I'm not saying any of that—

(Doug's beeper goes off, he checks it.)

SCOTT. Who is it? Trump or Rockefeller?
DOUG. It's not important...Trump. Anyway, we need to resolve this...if I've been hurtful, I want to change. I mean, we have to keep seeing each other, we have no choice.
SCOTT. I'm making it my choice.
DOUG. We can't stop seeing each other.
SCOTT. Yes, we can.
DOUG. Scott—we're brothers! Think about it. Christmas? Thanksgiving—I mean even if you want to stop these lunches or going to the same parties, it's kind of inevitable.

(Scott produces a document.)

SCOTT. That's why I had my lawyer-
DOUG. How can you afford a lawyer?
SCOTT. Pro-bono. Anyway—here is a restraining order. In respects to parties of mutual friends, blah-blah-blah, oh, here-either party, meaning us, not the party-party, who ever arrives first may remain for the first half of said party and the second party, person party, not party party, will attend the second half. Or this can be agreed upon via the phone twenty-four hours before

said party to be agreed upon by said parties.

DOUG. Have you fucking flipped?

SCOTT. Now, in respects to family gatherings, blah, blah, blah-yeah-said parties must maintain a footage deference zone of at least fifteen feet.

DOUG. Footage deference zone? This is lawyer talk?

SCOTT. Well, he's second year law-but he's very bright. But don't try to-

DOUG. What about dinner? The table is six feet long for Christ's sake.

SCOTT. Ah...*(Scanning.)*—for the sake of dietary intake in the form of familiar consumption designated as dinner, luncheons, or breakfast-snacks would have to be mutually agreed upon and amended, both parties agree to avoid direct conversational confrontation and maintain civility in an attempt to uphold the appearance of a focused-functional and coherent family force.

DOUG. You gotta be joking me.

SCOTT. If you'll just sign here, there's a Kinko's around the corner, I can get it notarized.

DOUG. I'm not going to sign that. I wouldn't even consider signing something as completely ludicrous as this. You are my only brother. I will let nothing come between us, and I won't leave this spot until this is rectified. *(Doug's beeper goes off and he checks it.)* Oh—I gotta take this.

(DOUG crosses off left as the waiter ENTERS with a large bowl of vodka and a mug of beer and puts them down.)

WAITER. So, you two straighten things out?

SCOTT. No...

WAITER. He coming back?

SCOTT. I don't know.

WAITER. You're too good for him, anyway.

SCOTT. Thanks...

WAITER. You gonna need a little more time?

SCOTT. Yeah... *(The waiter exits off left as Scott looks over the document.)* I'm gonna need a little more time...

BLACKOUT

ONE LAST TIME

ONE LAST TIME

One Last Time was a national winner of
Heartlad Theater Company's
"Parlor Plays" Ten Minute Play Competition

One Last Time premiered
at
Heartland Theater Company
Jun 12th, 2002
Directed By Mike Dobbins
featuring
Hosia Brown and Michael Hallahan

The genders of the two characters can be altered
for casting purposes.

The author takes place in the rear alley of a
funeral home.

Characters:
Allen/ Ellen
James/ Janet

(Lights up on an alleyway. ALLEN, a man in his late twenties or thirties, wearing an ill-fitting suit and carrying a briefcase, stares at a closed door. After a second, he turns to go as the door opens, revealing JAMES, a smartly dressed man in a dark suit dragging out a garbage can. He starts to leave but spies ALLEN. Directors note: when Allen speaks, it is clear he has some type of developmental problems.)

JAMES. Oh, Hello.
ALLEN. Hi....
JAMES. Are you here for the viewing?
ALLEN. The viewing?
JAMES. The service?
ALLEN. The service?
JAMES. For the deceased?
ALLEN. Oh...yeah...
JAMES. ...would you like to come in?
ALLEN. Inside?
JAMES. That's where everyone else is...
ALLEN. Everyone else?
JAMES. Yes-there's quite a few people in there already.
ALLEN. I didn't think anyone knew him...like me.
JAMES. Oh yes, he seems to have touched many people.
ALLEN. Really?... I thought I was his only friend.
JAMES. I'm sure, in your own way... your friendship was unique.
ALLEN. Unique?
JAMES. Special.
ALLEN. Oh...
JAMES. Do I know you?
ALLEN. I don't think so.
JAMES. Don't you work at the Dunkin' Donuts? On Park Street?
ALLEN. YEAH... I'm a mopper - well, I also sweep but mostly a mopper.
JAMES. Right.

(ALLEN starts pulling crumbled bills from his pocket.)

ALLEN. ...I, I uh wanna pay-
JAMES. That's quite generous of you, but the family has requested that in lieu of flowers, donations can be made to charities in his name.
ALLEN. What family?
JAMES. The deceased's family.

ALLEN. How did - how did they know?

JAMES. I - I'm sure someone contacted them...There's plenty of room inside if you'd like -

ALLEN. Did - did they pick out a casket? Because I don't think I could do that.

JAMES. Yes, they did - -it's all taken care of, like I said.

ALLEN. So, I don't get to do anything.

JAMES. I'm sure you'd be welcome inside-

ALLEN. I knew him better than all of them.

JAMES. I'm sure-

ALLEN. When he got hit by that man in the car - two years ago - it was me who took him to the doctor - it was me... and he stayed with me for three months - three whole months.

JAMES. I didn't know he had been in an accident.

ALLEN. Not a lot of people did...I was like the only person who talked to him. Really talked to him.

JAMES. You worked with him?

ALLEN. What? No- he was my friend.

JAMES. Yes, you said that... You were neighbors?

ALLEN. Yes - of course...jeez...

(ALLEN rolls his eyes like JAMES is slow or something.)

JAMES. Well, I need to get back inside...I can't really leave this door unlocked, for security reasons, but you're welcome to come around and inside when you're ready.

ALLEN. No.

*(ALLEN crosses over and places the briefcase on the garbage can. He opens
    the case for JAMES, who approaches unsuspectingly.)*

JAMES. If you - HOLY Mother of Pearl-what is that?

ALLEN. Fred.

JAMES. Is that rat?

ALLEN. NO...it's a squirrel.

JAMES. A dead squirrel?

ALLEN. I wouldn't bring a live squirrel to a funeral.

(Again Allen rolls his eyes.)

JAMES. I'm sorry - I thought you were here for the Seton viewing. That's what's going on inside right now.

ALLEN. No... I came here for him... I want to do the right thing.

JAMES. You would like a funeral for your friend, Fred? Is he a pet?

ALLEN. No - I told you he was friend. Weren't you listening?

JAMES. How... how do you know that that is Fred?

ALLEN. He only has a stub for a tail. He lost it when he got hit by a car two years ago. The pet doctor couldn't put it back on but helped him live... but now he's dead... I don't know why he's dead.

JAMES. I'm sorry...

ALLEN. Would you know why he's dead?

JAMES. No, I... sometimes... bad things happen.

ALLEN. I guess... But I want to do the right thing.

JAMES. We - we don't handle people's pets-

ALLEN. I already told you he wasn't a pet - he was a friend.

JAMES. Right.

ALLEN. If he was a pet, I'd have a leash and he'd know to avoid cars and still have his tail and maybe not be dead.

JAMES. Okay, okay.

ALLEN. He was my only real friend... he was a good listener... it's hard to find a good listener.

(JAMES sizes up ALLEN, the briefcase, and then pulls two latex gloves from his back pocket. He puts the gloves on and pulls an old bag from the top of the trash can.)

JAMES. I have to get back to the viewing but if you can come back tomorrow, say around six?

ALLEN. I get off at six - - can it be 6:05?

JAMES. Sure.

(JAMES gently places the unseen squirrel into the bag and closes the briefcase with his elbow.)

JAMES. We can hold a viewing at 6:05 tomorrow. I have a lovely Cohiba Rusto, oak... sarcophagus that I think would be perfect for Fred.

(ALLEN pulls the money from his pocket and counts.)

ALLEN. ...I don't have a lot of money-but I can mop for you. I can sweep too but I'm mostly a mopper.

JAMES. How much do you have?

ALLEN. I only have eight dollars and sixty-three cents.

JAMES. If we drop the traditional scented candles tribute, then it comes to eight sixty-three exactly.

ALLEN. Really?

JAMES. Yes...So...We'll see you tomorrow.

ALLEN. Okay...You're not going to cut him are you?

JAMES. I wouldn't think of it.

ALLEN. In the movies they fill them full of formal hide.

JAMES. That's the movies-I wont' do that to your sq..friend.

ALLEN. Uh...okay-see you tomorrow.

JAMES. Tomorrow then.

ALLEN. Thank you.

JAMES. You're welcome.

ALLEN. Would you like me to bring you a coffee? I get them free.

JAMES. Sure...milk with two sugars, please.

ALLEN. I won't forget...

(ALLEN turns and starts off. He stops.)

ALLEN. *(Cont.)* It'll be good to see him one last time... Boy could he jump.

JAMES. I'm sure.

ALLEN. But his best part... he was a good listener... A real good listener...

JAMES. They're hard to come by.

ALLEN. I know.

(ALLEN shuffles off and JAMES watches him go as the lights fade to black.)

THE GATE

THE GATE

The Gate was first produced
by
Shadowbox Cabaret
of Cincinnati Ohio
March, 1996
Directed by RJ Tolan
Featuring
Mathew Hahn, David Whitehouse, and Chris Hall

Action takes place on an empty stage, painted all white, with a
large white iron gate center stage.

Characters:
John
Mel
Pizzaboy/ Granny/ UPS Guy

(Lights up on MEL, a portly, non-descript, fella dressed in white coveralls. His shoes, cap and shirt are all white, as is his tool belt and tools. He casually whistles as he paints the large gate before him, which is, of course, white. JONATHAN, the yuppie, ENTERS from stage left. He's wearing only one shoe. He cautiously approaches Mel.)

JOHN. Excuse me.
MEL. Yeah?
JOHN. I uh, I seem to uh - am I in the right place?

(MEL puts down his paint brush and picks up a large white telephone book.)

MEL. Name?
JOHN. John - Jonathan Sears.
MEL. Sears... Sears... lemme see...Ketchum, Lawrence, Shirley MacClaine, Shirley MacClaine, Shirley MacClaine, Shirley MacClaine, Rolson, Samuels... Nope. Sorry.

(He closes the book.)

JOHN. Oh.
MEL. *(Pointing.)* You can catch the bus to hell right over there.
JOHN. Oh. *(JOHN turns to leave. MEL returns to painting. JOHN turns back.)* Um - could you look under the Balstookis?
MEL. What?
JOHN. Clarence Balstookis? Please? I, uh changed it when I moved to New York.
MEL. Oh, one of them. *(MEL rolls his eyes, picks up the book and re-reads.)* Balstookis...Yeah okay, you're here.
JOHN. Great! Then I guess I just go in?
MEL. Uh-oh.
JOHN. What - what's the matter?
MEL. You got an asterisk.
JOHN. What?

(JOHN attempts to look in the book but MEL pulls away.)

MEL. Hey, back off!
JOHN. I was just - what's an asterisk - by my name... what's that mean?
MEL. You're gonna have to wait.

JOHN. Why - for who?

MEL. For Peter - he's on break right now.

JOHN. But I'm on the list.

MEL. But you got an asterisk.

JOHN. Can I talk to Jesus, maybe? Straighten this thing out?

MEL. Jesus don't work the gates, he just does the sitting on the right side stuff. Besides, he's at lunch right now with Dahmer.

JOHN. Jeffrey Dahmer?

MEL. Yeah, you know him?

JOHN. Not personally...How'd he get in?

MEL. Connections - besides he had a great excuse. The "diminished capacity" route - The big G's a real softie on that one. Bein' sick in the head is different from being sick in your heart.

JOHN. Well - maybe 1 should talk to him - the big G?

MEL. Yeah, right.

JOHN. Look - I —

MEL. HEY! You're gonna have to wait.

JOHN. If you'd let me in-

MEL. I have no authority to let you through them gates. You're gonna have to wait.

(MEL returns to his painting.)

JOHN. Fine.

(JOHN crosses down left to sit on a bench. As he is about to sit, MEL, without looking in that direction, speaks.)

MEL. I wouldn't sit there if I was you.

JOHN. Why?

MEL. Because that, young man, is the bench for the bus stop to hell. The big D swings around an sees ya copping a seat, he'll put you on his bus.

(JOHN walks back over to MEL.)

JOHN. So this is heaven, huh?

MEL. No, it's Iowa. Kevin Kostner is over in that cornfield behind third base taking a dump.

JOHN. I don't see any cornfield.

MEL. Let me guess - you were a systems analyst?

JOHN. Lawyer.
MEL. That's a first.

(MEL resumes painting.)

JOHN. Painting the gates, huh?
MEL. You sure you're not a systems analyst?
JOHN. I always thought they were made of gold.
MEL. That would be vain.
JOHN. Wait a minute - Pearly gates - maybe it was pearl.
MEL. That would be gauche.
JOHN. *(Looking around.)* So... white is in, huh?
MEL. The color is different to every new applicant.
JOHN. Applicant? *(MEL returns to his painting.)* Applicant - wait a minute - I'm in - I'm on the list!
MEL. You had an asterisk!
JOHN. Well, when Mr. Peter shows, we'll straighten this out.
MEL. Sure we will.
JOHN. Why are you being so hostile?
MEL. Because I'm the janitor here, not a waiter, not a secretary and not a message taker. I don't got all the time in the world to explain everything to you. All your questions should've been answered in the pamphlet.
JOHN. What pamphlet?
MEL. The Death Pamphlet.
JOHN. I didn't get one.
MEL. That's impossible.
JOHN. I didn't get one.
MEL. That's a first.
JOHN. Maybe that was what the asterisk meant.
MEL. Hmph.

*(Suddenly, a loudly dressed teenager on a skateboard and carrying a pizza
box rolls up to MEL and JOHN.)*

KID. Hey, how's it going? I got a pizza here for a Mr. Jesus.
MEL. Beat it.
KID. It's a pepperoni, peppers and -
MEL. I said beat it, kid.
KID. Hey, buddy, if I don't deliver this, it comes out of my paycheck. And if this Mr. Jesus doesn't get his pie - somebody's gonna catch some

serious-

MEL. Hey! The big J ordered no pizza! Move on, punk!

KID. Well, here. Take it, forget about it.

MEL. Please, don't insult my intelligence.

JOHN. Hey, I'll take it off your hands -

(JOHN reaches for his wallet. The kid smiles and offers the pizza to JOHN.)

MEL. Don't touch that pizza, Balstookis.

JOHN. What's the big deal. I'm hungry, the kid's in a jam -

(As JOHN reaches for the box, MEL intercedes, slapping his hand down and faces the kid.)

MEL. Begone... before I honk the big G.

(The kid frowns, flips MEL the bird and skates off, pizza in hand. JOHN picks up his wallet in confusion.)

JOHN. What the hell was that all about?

MEL. Exactly.

JOHN. What?

MEL. That was "the hell."

JOHN. Help me out here.

MEL. That was him.

JOHN. WHO?!!

MEL. Mephistopheles, the dark one, Beelzebub, Succubus, Old Nick, Old Gooseberry, Old Scratch, the BIG D!

JOHN. *(Pointing.)* The big D?

MEL. The one and only.

JOHN. Delivering pizza?

MEL. One of the oldest tricks in the book. He'll try anything to get through these gates.

JOHN. Does Jesus even like pizza?

MEL. Loves the stuff. Why do you think he put the Vatican in Italy?

JOHN. This is all so-

MEL. A lot to take in - I know. *(JOHN sits down on the ground. MEL crosses and sits with him.)* Sorry I got rough with you, but he's pretty tricky, comes pokin' around lookin' for stragglers or a chance to sneak in.

JOHN. Why doesn't he just hop the fence?

MEL. Can't do it. Has to be invited in. Now you see why we gotta be tough at the door. Nothing personal.

(MEL pulls a pack of cigarettes out of his pocket and lights one up. He offers the pack to JOHN.)

JOHN. No thanks, those suckers will kill - oh... sure, what the-
MEL. Hey - the language!
JOHN. Oh, sorry. Thanks.

(JOHN takes a cigarette and MEL lights it up.)

MEL. Couple o' words the Big G don't allow to be said around here. That's one of them.
JOHN. And the others?
MEL. *(Listing them on his fingers.)* Rayon, Scud, Moonies, and Quayle. All these are mistakes created by man, and a big ole itch in his caboose. If you bump into him inside - steer clear of those.
JOHN. I get an audience with him?
MEL. No, you do not! But you might bump into him on the course. It's a beauty. Course, he gets to walk across the water hazards. And by the way, he is always allowed to play through. Got it?
JOHN. I don't play golf.
MEL. You will. How'd you lose the shoe?
JOHN. Oh that. I guess it popped off when I was hit by the street sweeper.
MEL. Whereabouts?
JOHN. Columbus Circle - it's a very tricky intersection to cross.
MEL. Obviously.
JOHN. I was heading across and spied a penny face up on the street.
MEL. And?
JOHN. Well, if you pick up a penny face up, it's good luck. Unfortunately, this one had been kinda pushed into the surface - so as I tried to pry it up with my fingers, I didn't notice the street cleaner bearing down on me.
MEL. Some lucky penny.
JOHN. Yep... So, let me get this straight. You work here?
MEL. Yep.
JOHN. So you have to work up here?
MEL. No, you don't have to. I do it cause I enjoy it. See down on the big W, I had a very destructive existence. Up here I get a chance to build, create.
JOHN. What did you do before?

MEL. Kill people.

JOHN. Kill people.

MEL. I was a hit man.

JOHN. A hit man.

MEL. Yep.

JOHN. This is quite enlightening.

MEL. Not what you expected.

JOHN. Not what I expected.

MEL. *(Standing.)* Yeah, well - you're not the first to say that. You shoulda seen Charley Manson's face when he showed up.

JOHN. Charles Manson is up here ?! Wait, don't tell me - "diminished capacity."

MEL. I think it was the swastika on the forehead that put him over the top. The Big G is a sucker for lost causes... But hey, who are we to judge? Charley's done alright - married Indira Ghandi last week.

JOHN. Get out of town!

MEL .Yep. Ghengis Kahn was the best man.

JOHN. Who doesn't get in here?

MEL. *(Dead serious.)* The dead souls, the unhallowed, the dark of heart. Head cases aren't necessarily denied entry.

JOHN. Well, buddy, I can assure you that I'm none of those-

MEL. But you got an asterisk.

JOHN. So I tore some tags off some pillows, c'mon-

MEL. *(Picking up the chart.)* Didn't say anything about no tags - better make a note.

JOHN. I was joking - really - I just, I don't know what the problem could be-

(The pizza delivery boy, disguised as an elderly woman ENTERS down left, interrupting JOHN. She makes it about halfway and stumbles. As she falls to the ground, JOHN rushes to her side.)

MEL. Don't do it.

WOMAN. Help! I've fallen, and I can't get up!

JOHN. Even I'm not stupid enough to buy that one. *(The lady hops up, shoots the two a mean glance, and steals off left.)* Does he do this all the time?

MEL. When he knows that stragglers are about. He must've gotten tipped off about your asterisk.

JOHN. Why am I the only person here?

MEL. Whad'ya mean?

JOHN. Well, I mean, you know - people are dying every second - car accidents, starvation, murder, war, plane crashes, floods-

MEL. Don't forget pestilence-

JOHN. Pestilence ... I figured there'd be a line that would shame a rock concert - where is everybody?

JOHN. The Big G don't believe in lines - he's able to adjust and alter time to fit his schedule. There's never a line.

JOHN. Cool.

MEL. But there are asterisks.

JOHN. I really have no clue what that could be.

MEL. You spank a lot as a teenager?

JOHN. Excuse me?

MEL. Hack your carrot - masturbate?

JOHN. Well I - no more than - could that keep me from getting in here?

MEL. *(Smiling.)* Nah -I just love askin' the question and watching some of you stiff shirts turn a shade.

JOHN. That's really not nice-

MEL. Well, I'm still working on the nice part of me - I'm a work in progress.

JOHN. I thought up here - everything's complete,

MEL. Who told you that?

JOHN. I don't know - the Bible?

MEL. Oh yeah - that's another thing - don't bring that up once you're inside the big H.

JOHN. Why?

MEL. Let's just say a couple of ancient Shakespeares took it upon themselves to speak for the Big G. Even after two thousand years, it's still a thorn in his side.

JOHN. God holds a grudge?

MEL. It's not for us to say how or what the Big G feels, but he can get annoyed. They've been kinda fuckin up big time down on the big W. A lot lately.

JOHN. Is that why there's so much evil in the world? He's annoyed?

MEL. Hold on there, you're getting way ahead of yourself. A lot of evil that exists down there is man made - wars, vehicular accidents - be it plane, train, automobile-

JOHN. What about acts of God?

MEL. Now, that's a real nasty term made up by the evilest of entities.

JOHN. The big D?

MEL. The big I.

JOHN. Big I?

MEL. Insurance companies. Now for weather phenomena and tragedies of fate and misfortune, hey that's the luck of the draw. Why do they call it Tornado Alley - cause there's tornadoes. Don't build there. Why call it San Andreas Fault? You don't move there. You buy a house below sea level because you're head's up your ass? I mean c'mon. If man chooses to challenge forces he cannot control, he will not win. You do not build a baby's bed in a beehive, yet some fool will. He invites tragedy. You see, tragedy is not excess of evil, rather a lack of good, be it luck or nature.

JOHN. I don't think I follow you.

MEL. See, if the Big G babysat his creation to the point of negating bad occurrences, then there'd be no need for the upstairs. Bad things happen down there because the Big G gives us the freedom to make choices, to pursue options and live or die with the consequences. No strings, no nets, no back-up.

JOHN. So where does the big D fit into this?

MEL. He'll never know the foil story. He'll always lack the big G's approval. He'll never know what's behind those gates - the warmth, the contentness. That's what drives the big D -hunger for acceptance.

JOHN. So then hell is actually a lack of heaven?

MEL. Forever and ever - ad infinitum - kinda like knocking on the front door of the best party in town and never getting in.

JOHN. Wow.

*(A uniformed U.P.S. man ENTERS from down right and crosses to JOHN and
    MEL.)*

MAN. Got a package here for the big G.

MEL. I'll take it-

JOHN. Watch out!

*(As the MAN hands the package to MEL, JOHN swats it down and stomps on
    it furiously. MEL pushes JOHN off the box.)*

MEL. What are you doing?

JOHN. *(Breathlessly pointing at MAN.)* The big D! The big D!

MEL. John - he really is U.P.S. Really.

MAN. Sign here, please.

(MEL signs the MAN's clipboard and hands it back to him.)

MEL. What is it?
MAN. It was a cheesecake. Make sure receiver understands it was not damaged in transit.
MEL. Will do.
MAN. *(To JOHN.)* Hey, buddy-
JOHN. Yes?
MAN. Lighten up.

(The MAN EXITS as MEL picks up the stomped box to inspect it.)

JOHN. I... I'm sorry... maybe we can fix it.
MEL. Don't think so... you totalled this bad boy.
JOHN. Are you going to tell him?
MEL. Omnipotent - ring a bell?
JOHN. *(Sinking.)* Oh no...
MEL. Your heart was in the right place.
JOHN. It was - you're right - it was!
MEL. Don't sweat it, kiddo, I'll take care of it.
JOHN. Likes cheesecake, huh?
MEL. Can't get enough of the stuff.
JOHN. I love it too! Every time - oh ... oh no, oh boy.
MEL. What?
JOHN. Oh boy, oh I know-
MEL. What?
JOHN. The cheesecake... cheesecake.
MEL. What are you babbling about?
JOHN. I know what the asterisk is about!
MEL. Hey, take it easy. Get yourself together... want to tell me about it?
JOHN. Monday, September 30th, one-thirty-five in the afternoon... I know it's the asterisk.
MEL. Go on.
JOHN. I had just left Ethan's - a nice little bistro near the circle. Well, I had just had a lunch with a headhunter from another firm. It had really gone well. I mean I wasn't sure if I'd go with them but I was feeling pretty pumped from the session. He was stroking me royally... Anyway, I had ordered a piece of cheesecake for dessert, but it was huge, so I just wrapped it in my napkin to take back to the office.
MEL. Okay.

JOHN. So I come out of the restaurant and reach the corner. There's this lady -a dirty, smelly old woman dressed in tatters, bumming change from passersby. I put on my best non-tourist face and look straight ahead even though I know she's coming to me. Oooh, she stunk awful.

MEL. Uh-huh.

JOHN. So she starts hassling me, begging, some stupid little story. I shake my head gently and say, "I'm sorry," but she just wouldn't go away, and the light seemed to be taking forever, and then—

MEL. Tell me, John.

JOHN. She sticks her finger right into my cheesecake. I mean I watched in horror as her dirty, wrinkly finger punctured the napkin and dug deeply into that beautiful cheesecake. I was aghast. I was enraged.

MEL. What'd you do, John?

JOHN. I punched her - well, actually, I pushed her face with my hand - hard. I pushed her back and she fell onto the curb. I think she might have hurt something. I don't know. I wanted to kick her. I really felt violated. How dare she pull this shit. I'm a fucking taxpayer!

MEL. Did you kick her?

JOHN. No, but there was the hatred within me to do it... I threw the cheesecake down before her, smashed it with my shoe into the pavement, and then I spit on it... and then I spit on... I spit on her... I heard somebody cheering... and deep down I felt good about... I'm really sick of these people. Something has to be done. But I know that's it. That must be it.

MEL. I know that's it. I'm sure that's it.

JOHN. I shouldn't have done it.

MEL. You were pushed. You're only human. Do you regret it?

JOHN. I guess I should, shouldn't I.

MEL. Yes.

JOHN. I do.

MEL. I know you do. *(MEL puts his hand on JOHN'S shoulder, and then gently kisses JOHN on the forehead.)* You can go in now.

JOHN. I can? But I thought I had to wait.

MEL. No, you're free to enter.

JOHN. But... was this a test?

MEL. More of a screening process... go on.

JOHN. Okay...*(JOHN opens the gate and cautiously peers in. He turns back to MEL and smiles sheepishly.)* Just walk in?

MEL. Yep.

(JOHN walks in, closing the gate behind him and walks off left. MEL smiles

and produces a handkerchief. He removes his cap to wipe his brow. On his forehead protrude two small horns. He turns and smiles to the audience.)
MEL. *(Cont.)* I love this job.

(MEL EXITS through the gate.)

BLACKOUT

THE END

PROPERTY LIST

THE BLONDE

Single hanging light bulb (Should be practical)
Hand truck
Rope
Handcuffs
Handkerchief (for gag)

THANKSGETTING

Small formal dinner table (set for two)
Coatrack
Bottle of wine
2 chairs
Business card

FINAL APPROACH

Two chairs
Steering wheel (optional)

CLOSURE

Small formal dinner table (set for two)
cell phone
waiter's apron
waiter's order pad
Large bowl of water
legal papers
pen

ONE LAST TIME

Brick wall flat (with practical door)
full garbage bag
trash can
battered briefcase

THE GATE

Large white gate	park bench	UPS uniform (Brown pants,
paint brush	painter overalls	Brown shirt and hat)
walker or cane	paint can	paint brush
shawl	spectacles	large book
skateboard	pizza box	
grey wig	small package	

SHORT PLAYS FOR EVERY VENUE

THE BEQUEST by Dale Wasserman

Eyebrows rise in a small town when a notorious playboy dies leaving a large bequest to the lovely wife of a local reporter. "A polished miniature from a playwright better known for his blockbusters."—*What's On.* 3 m., 3 f.(#4267)

CELEBRATION by Harold Pinter

Diners and the staff at an elegant restaurant treat audiences to some unusually entertaining fare in this London hit by a major voice of the modern theatre. "[An] entire smorgasbord of gorgeous verbal moves."—*New Yorker.* 5 m., 4 f. (#5870)

THE JUICE OF WILD STRAWBERRIES
by Jean Lenox Toddie

A woman seeks renewal after loss in this touching play. "This gem celebrates life, love and the wisdom that comes with age."—Mill Mountain Theatre, Roanoke. 1 m., 1 f. (#12659)

MOSQUITO DIRIGIBLE AEROSOL DEODORANT
by Conrad E. Davidson

A professor who thinks he is a dirigible undergoes other transformations during therapy, even becoming a mosquito. Unfortunately, the psychiatrist has an obsessive fear ... of mosquitoes. 2 m., 2 f. (#15732)

REFUGEES by Stephanie Satie

The hearts and minds of new immigrants and refugees as they reinvent their lives in American are revealed in five scenes that are set over five weeks in an English as a Second Language class. 1 f. (to play 3 m., 7 f.) (#19773)

SLAVERY by Jonathan Payne

In the 1030's, the Federal Writer's Project interviewed former slaves who were then in their eighties, nineties and older. Here are some of these moving, first-hand narratives. Paired with traditional Negro spirituals, they offer dramatic insights into the human side of slavery. 3 m., 4 f. (#21521)

For the broadest selection of short plays in print, see
THE BASIC CATALOGUE OF PLAYS AND MUSICALS
online at www.samuelfrench.com

<u>**Recently Published One-Act Plays**</u>

THE AWARD AND OTHER PLAYS
Waren Manzi

One for the Money
Moroccan Travel Guide
The Queen of the Parting Shot
The Audition
The Award

CHERRY SODA WATER
THREE RELATED ONE-ACT PLAYS
Stephen Levi

Cherry and Little Banjo
Red Roses for My Lady
The Gulf of Crimson

CONTACT WITH THE ENEMY and **GETTING IN**
Frank Gilroy

DECISIONS, DECISIONS
Fred Carmichael

GENDERMAT
Mark Dunn

GUARDING THE BRIDGE
Chuck Gordon

LUNACY: A BATHROOM TRILOGY
Richard Tuttle

The Lunatic from Number Seven
Sing a Pretty Song
Search and Rescue

OFFICE SUITE
Alan Bennett

A Visit from Miss Prothero
Green Forms